# Adult Coloring Book

# Lion & Lionese

Bambang Wisudyantoro

cannonzhooter@gmail.com

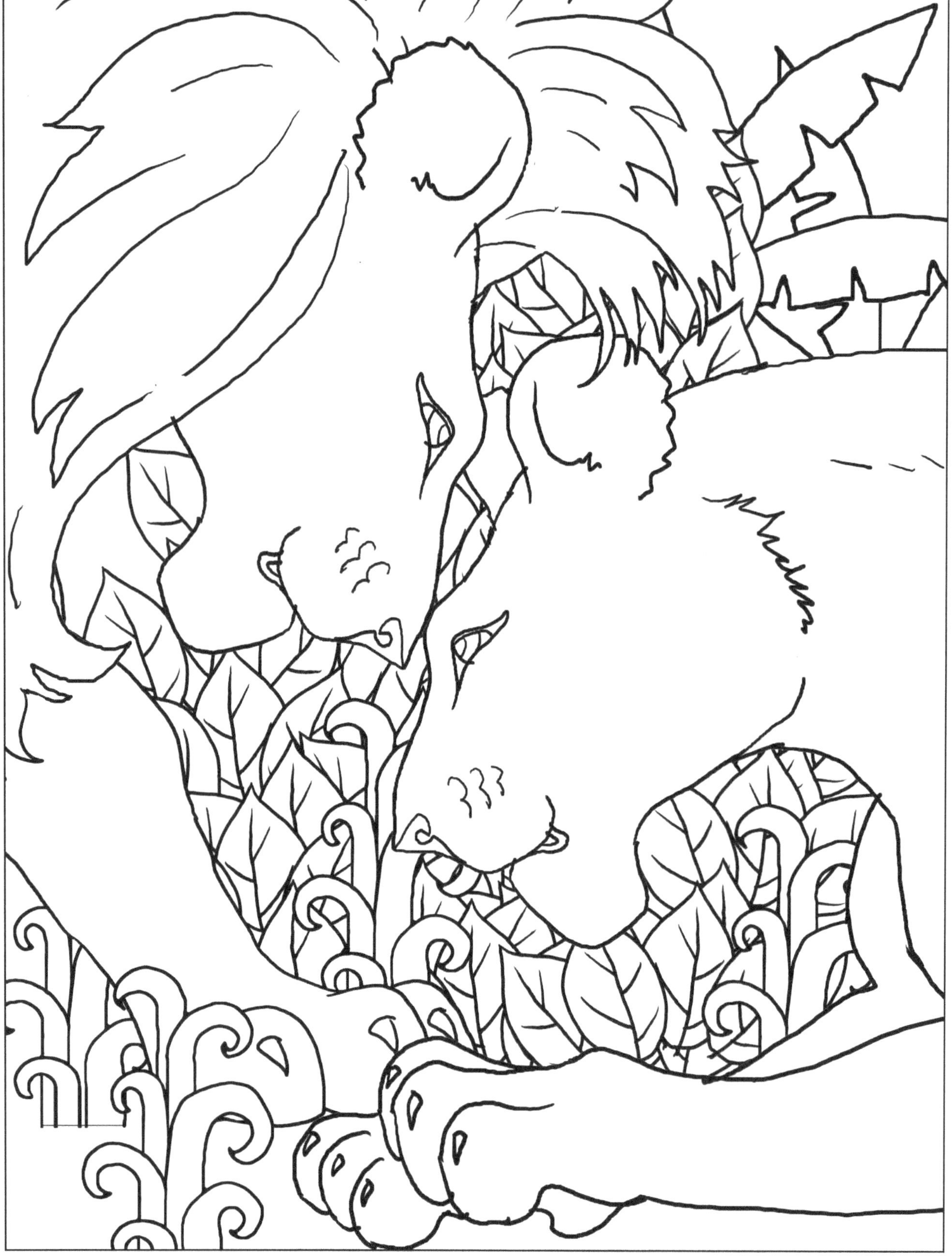

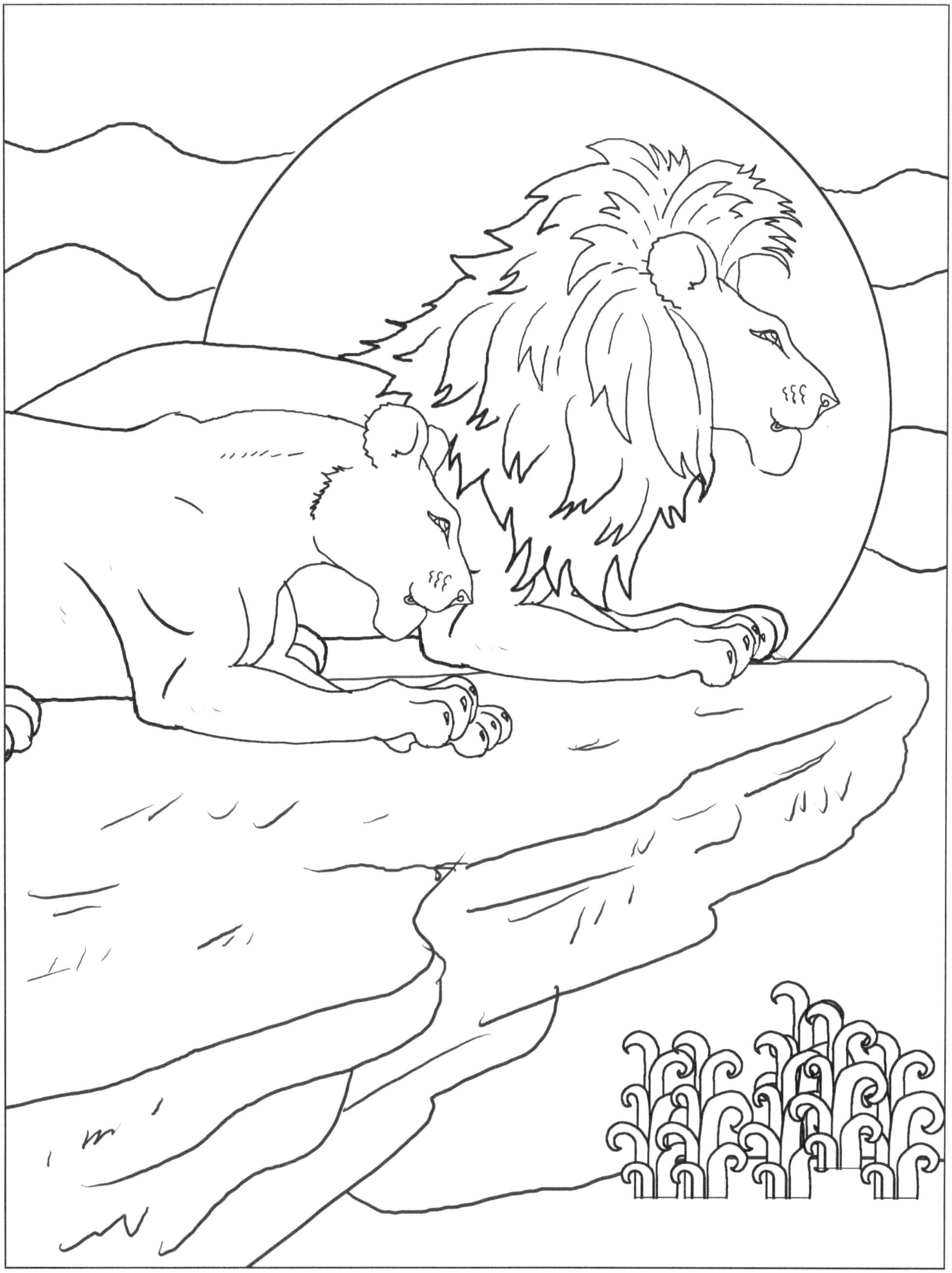

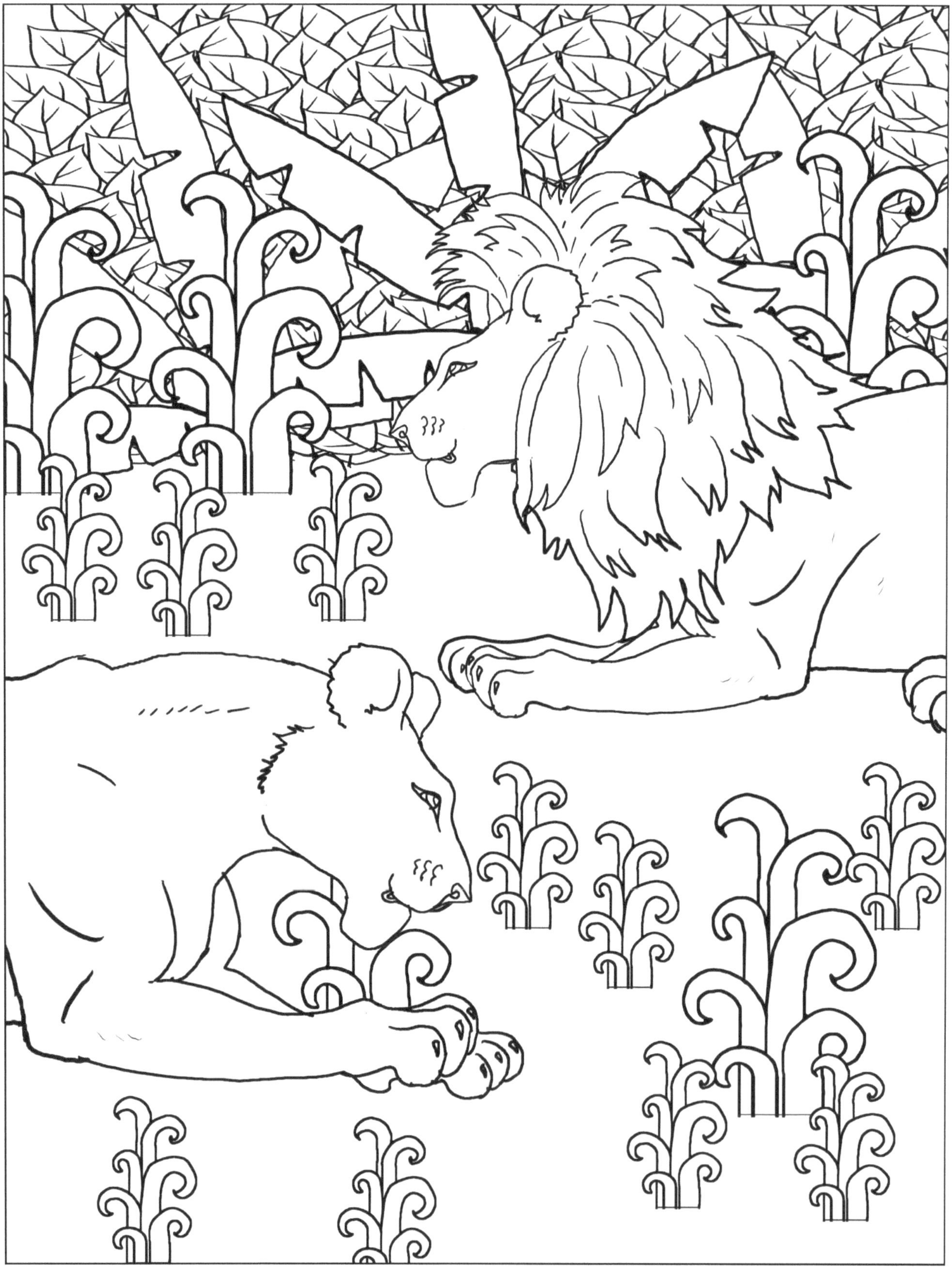

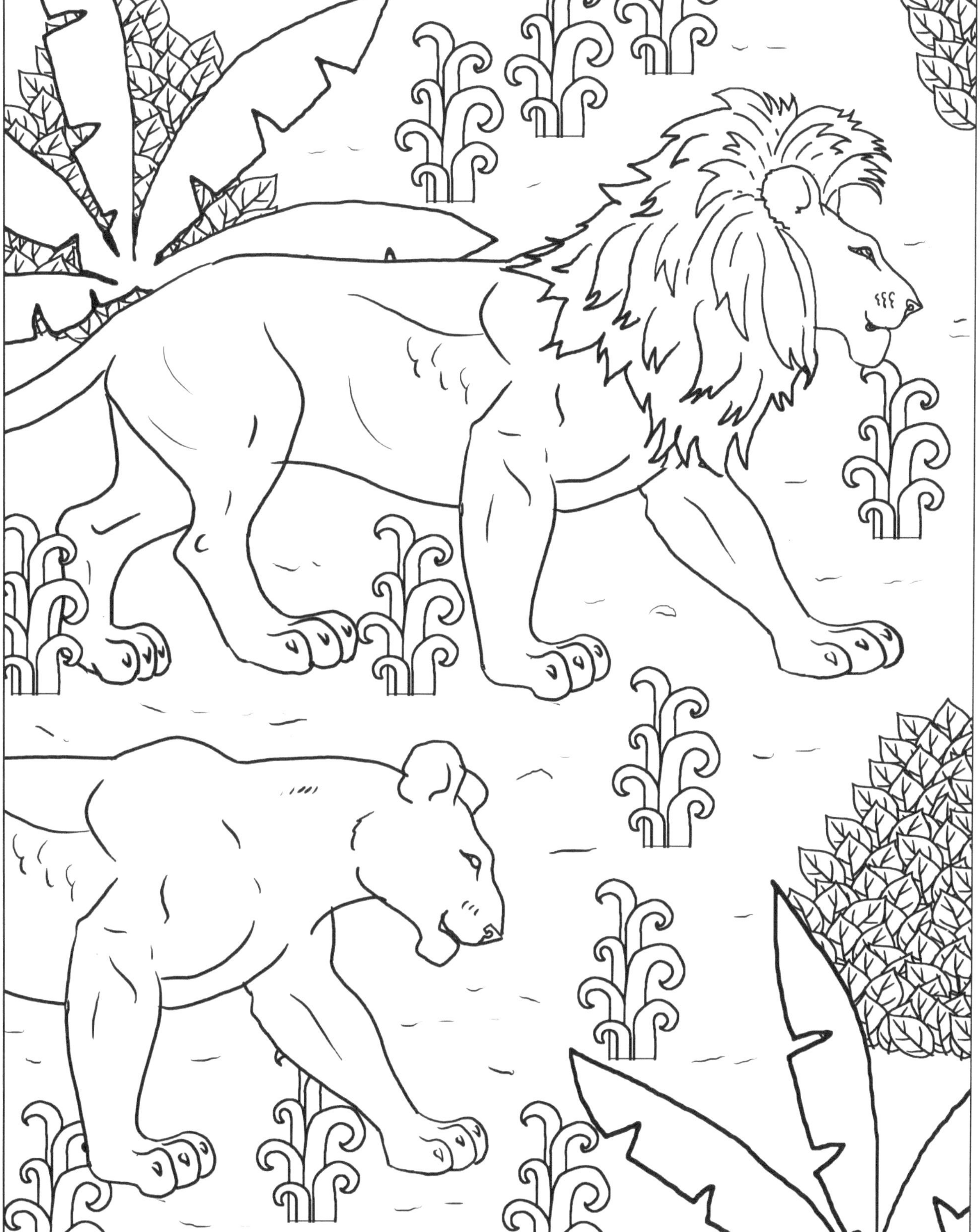

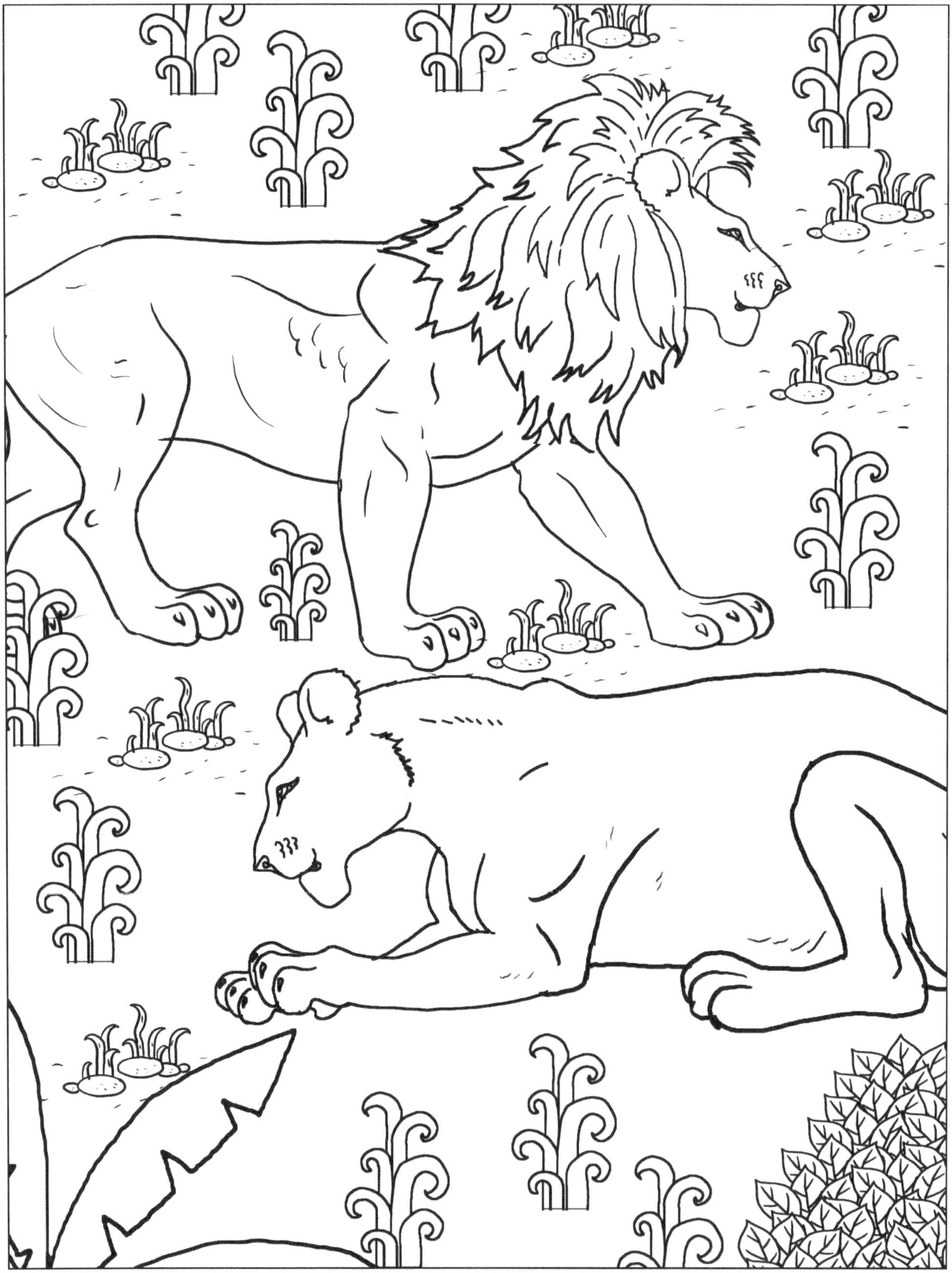

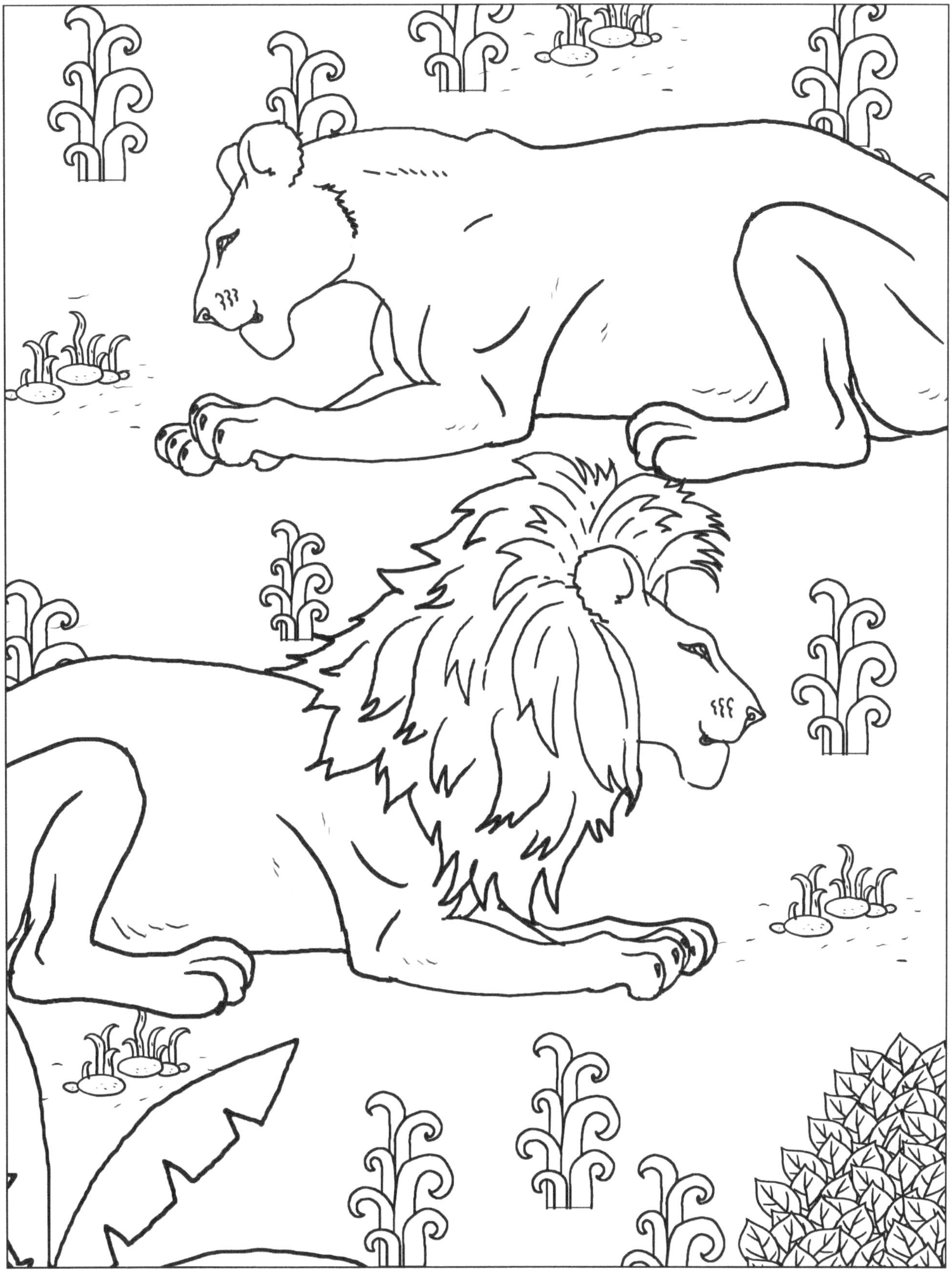

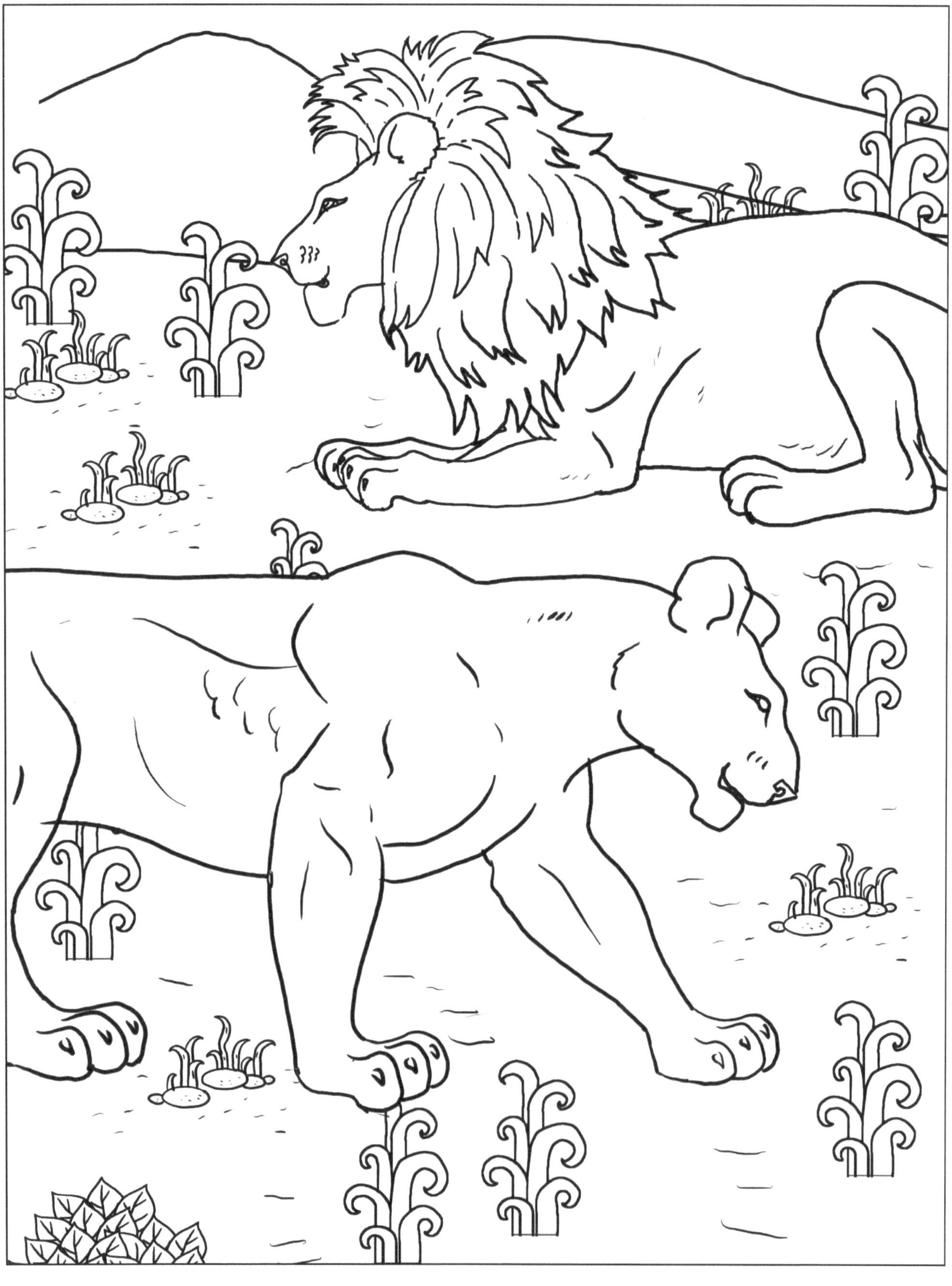

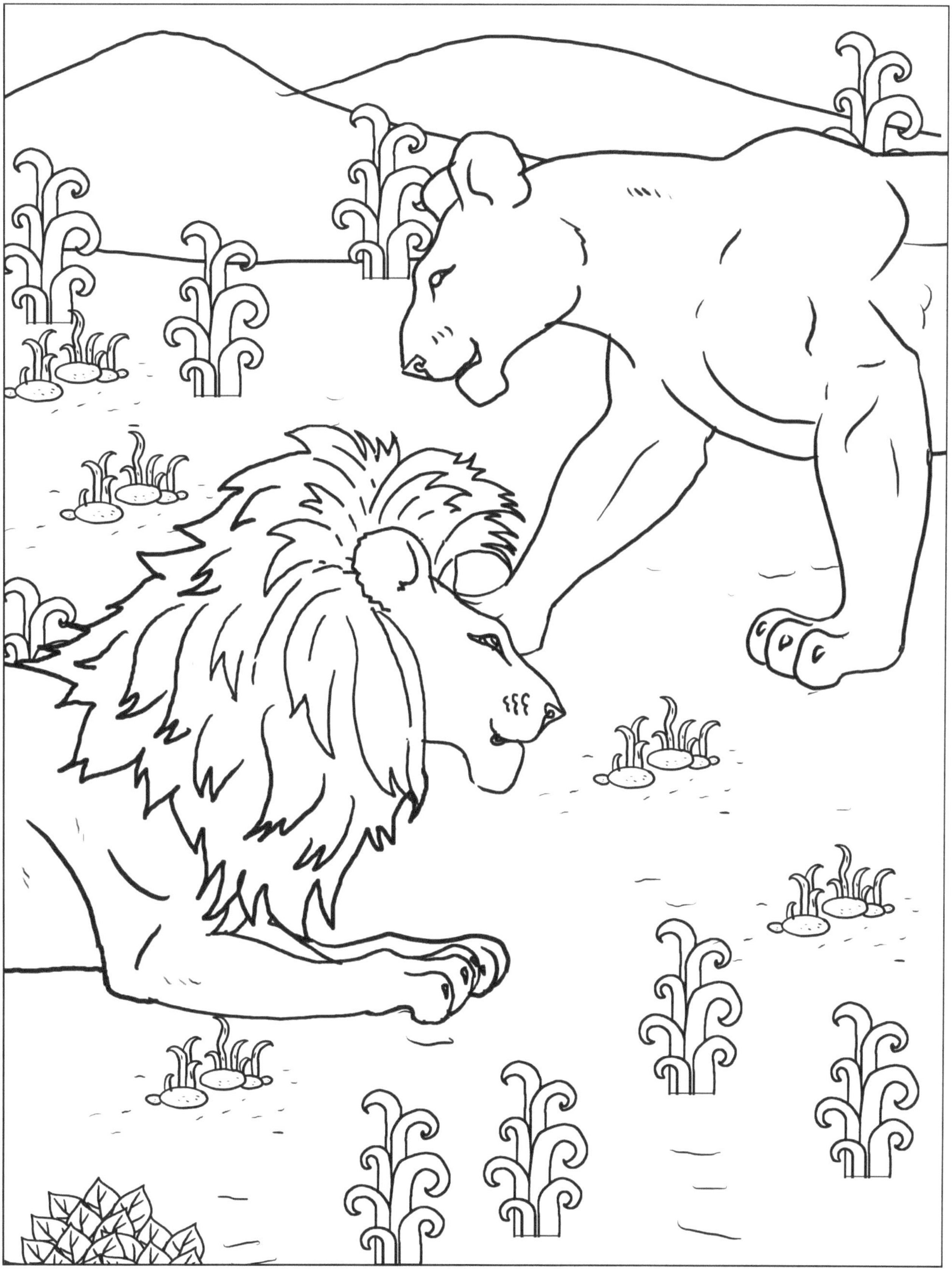

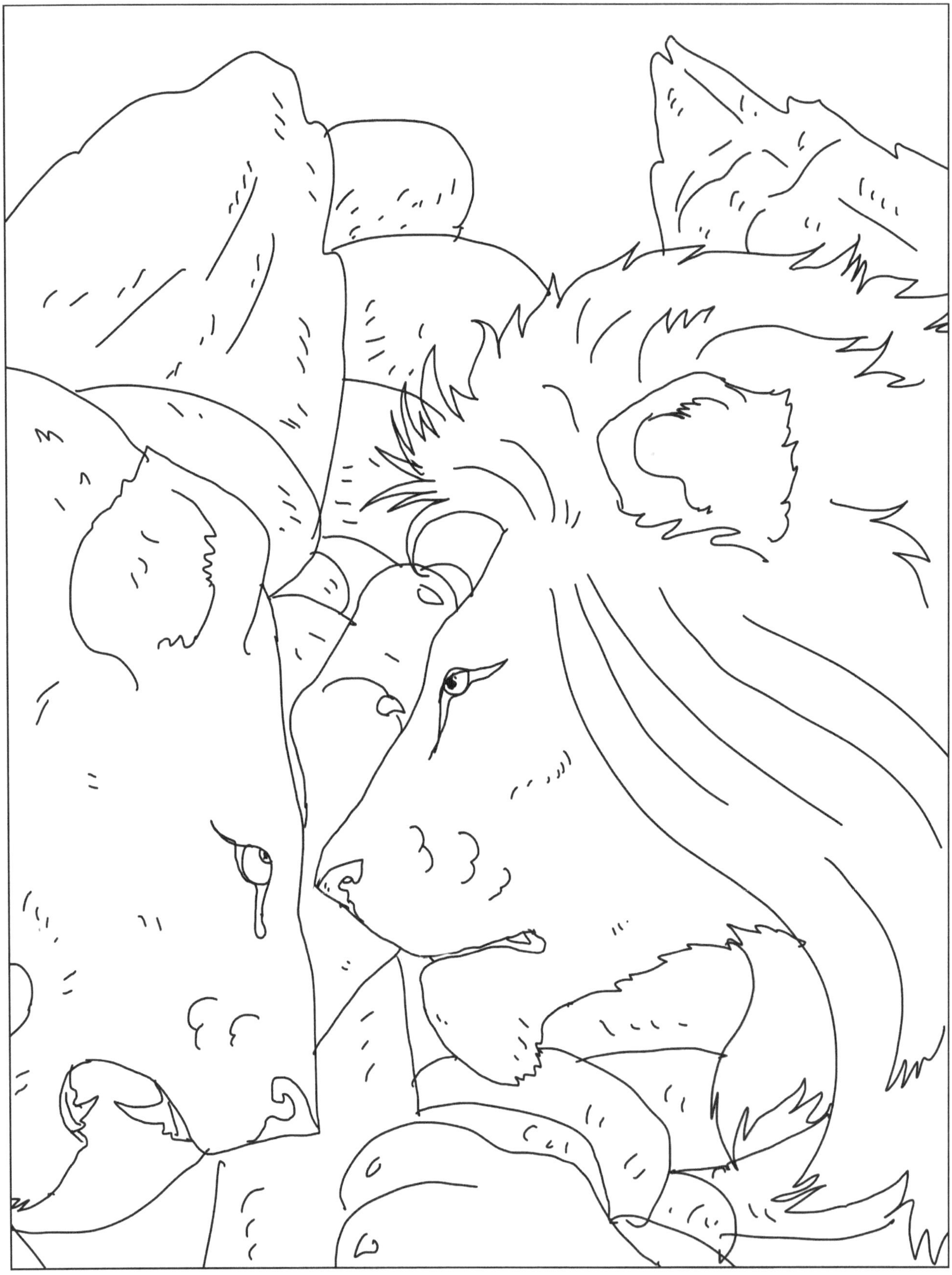

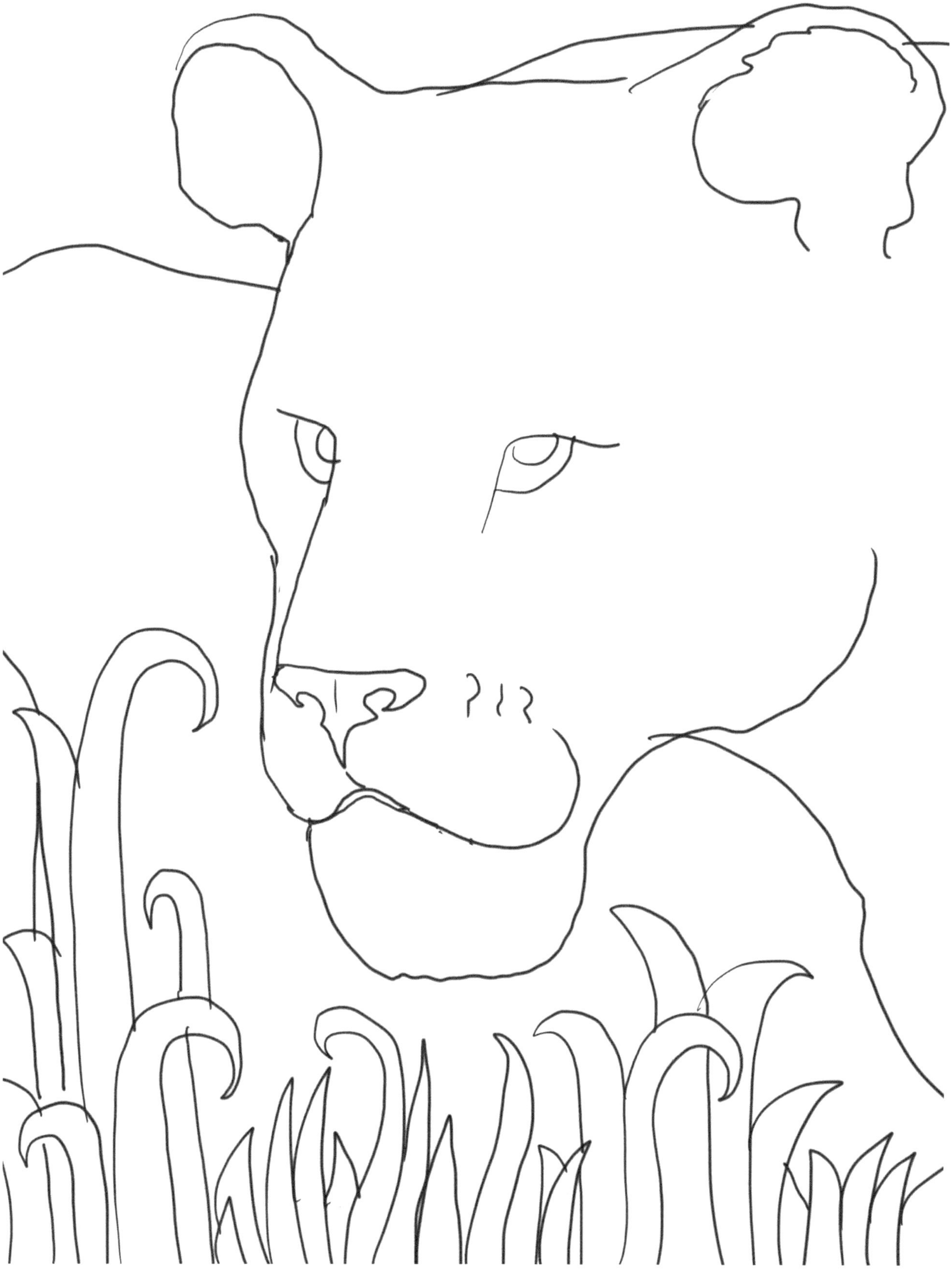

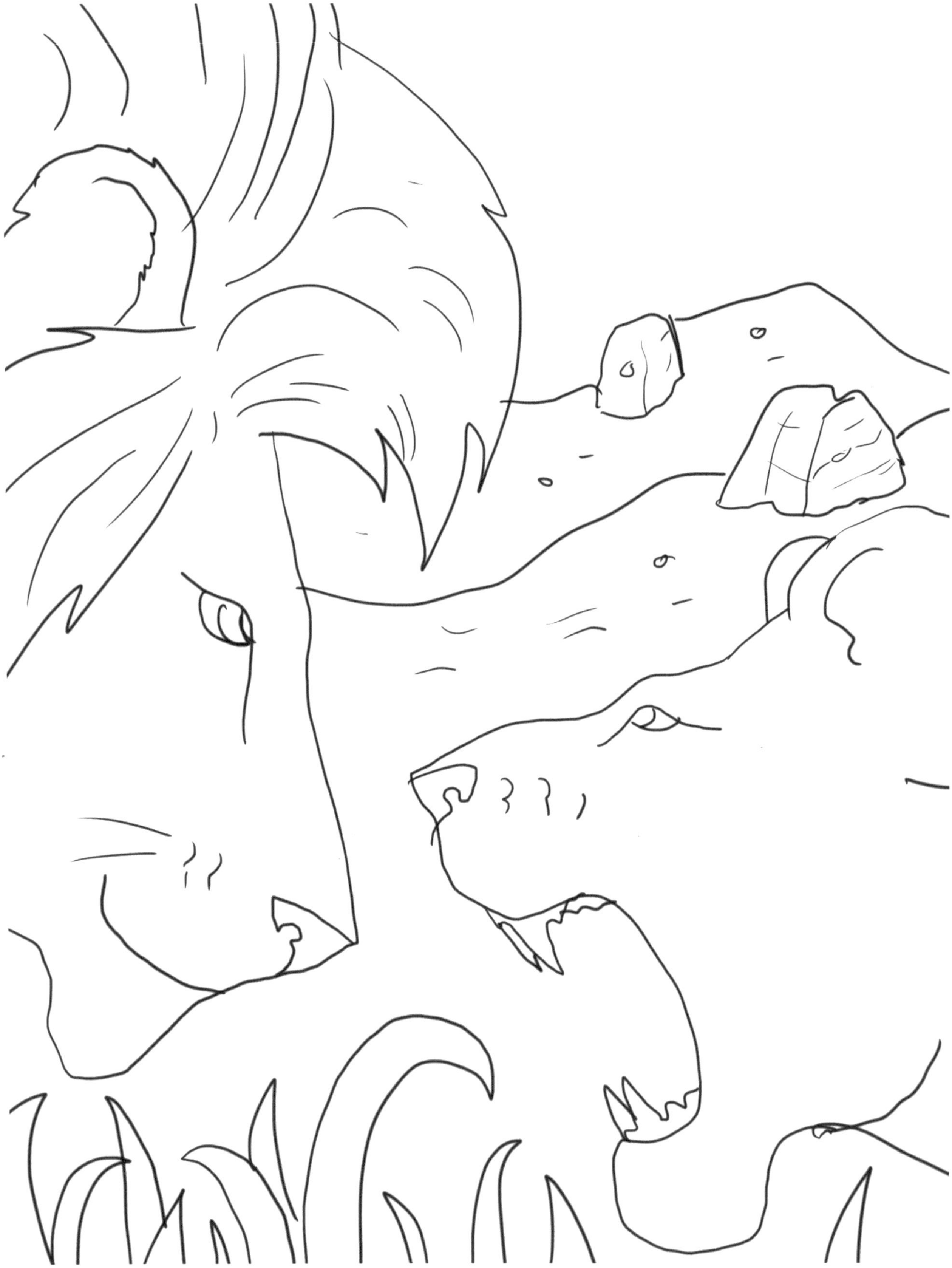

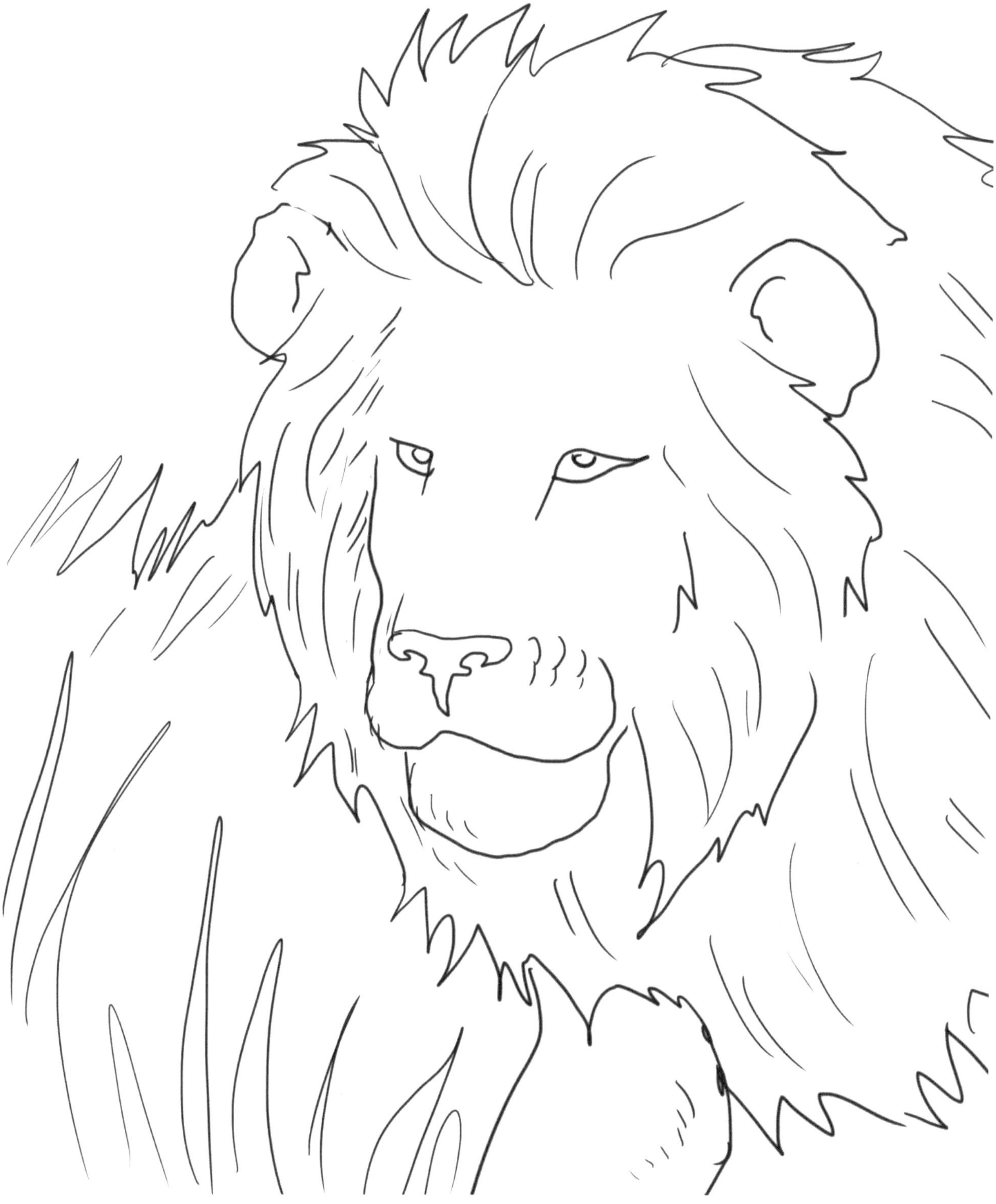

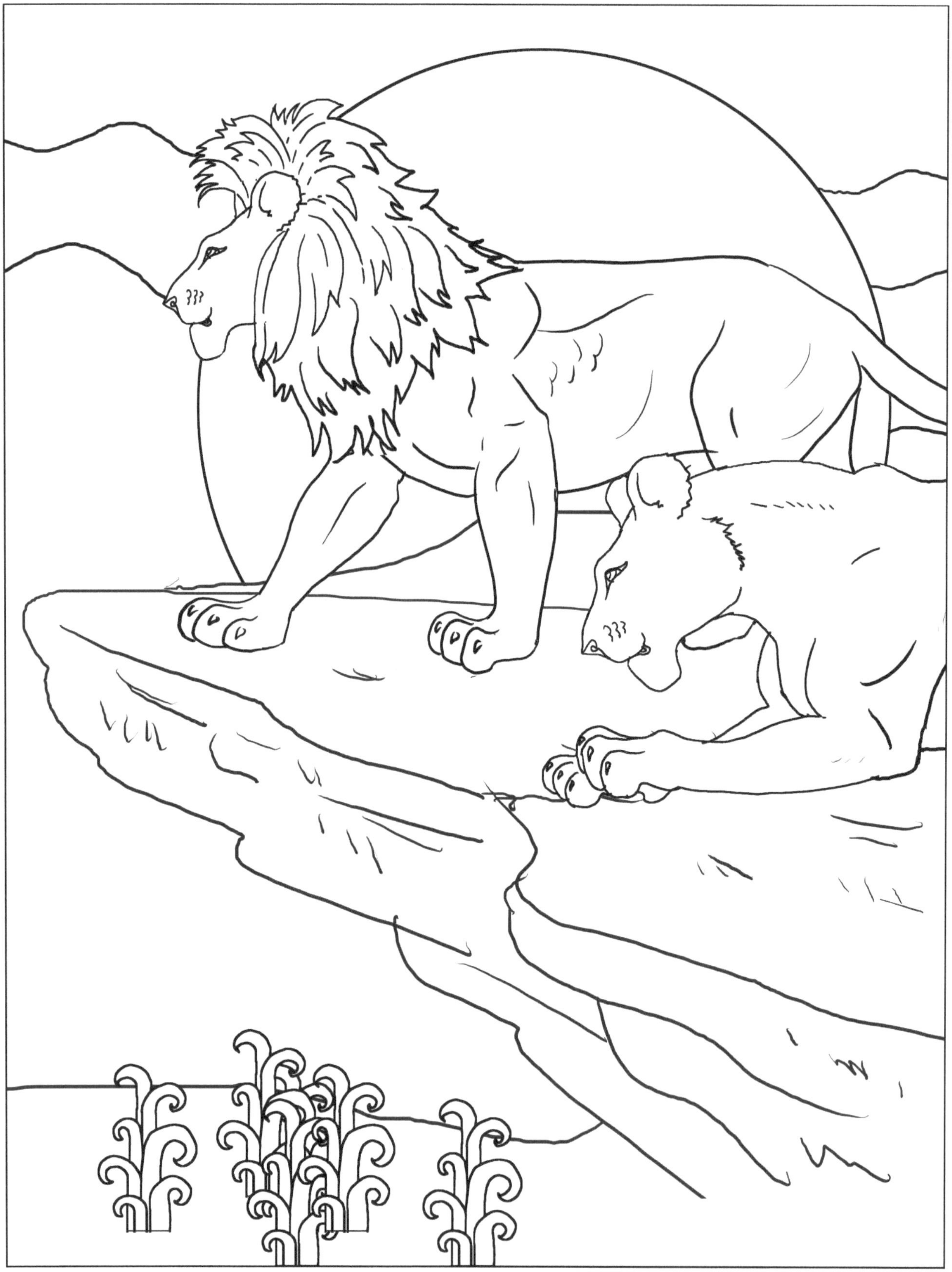

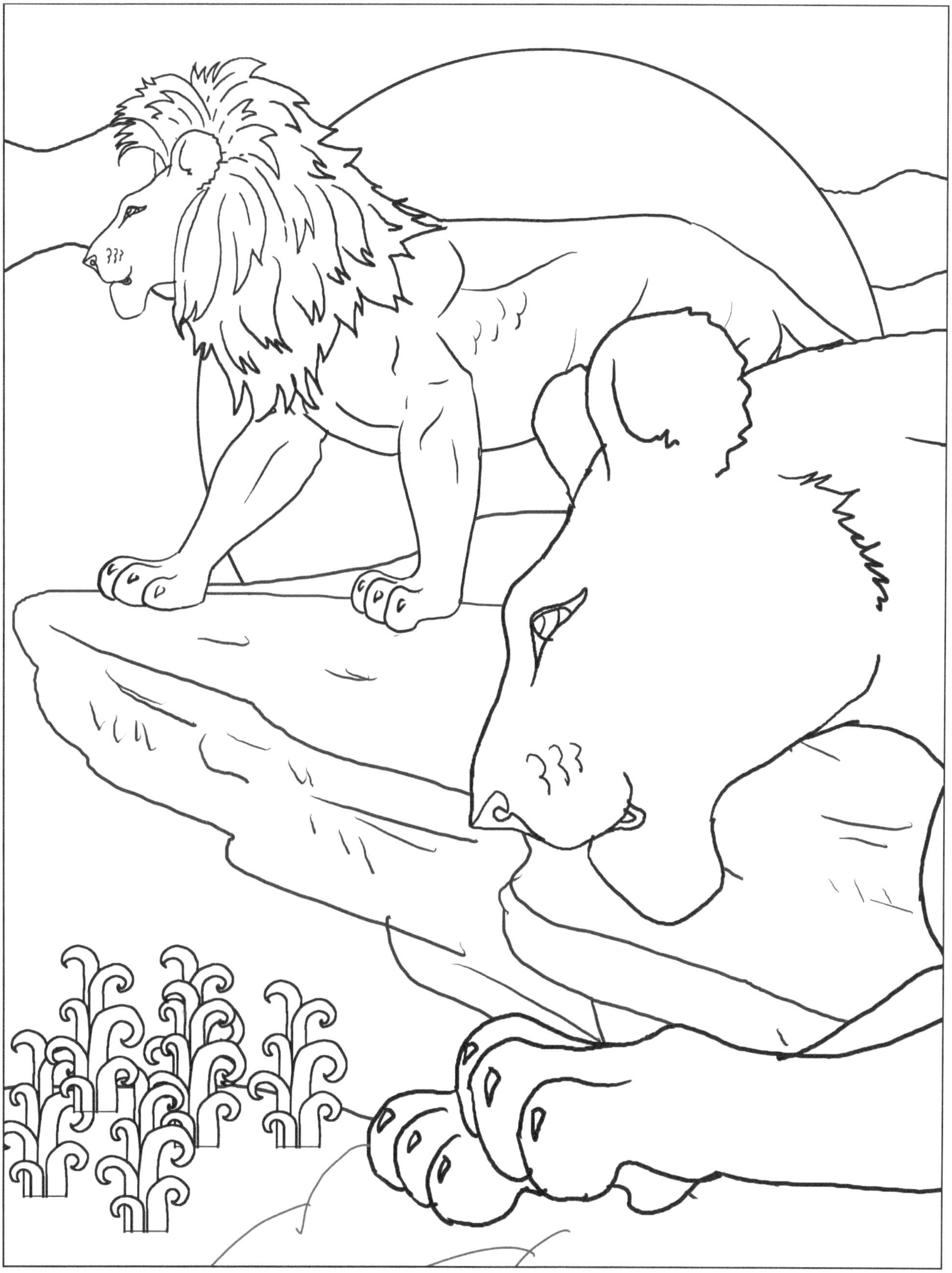

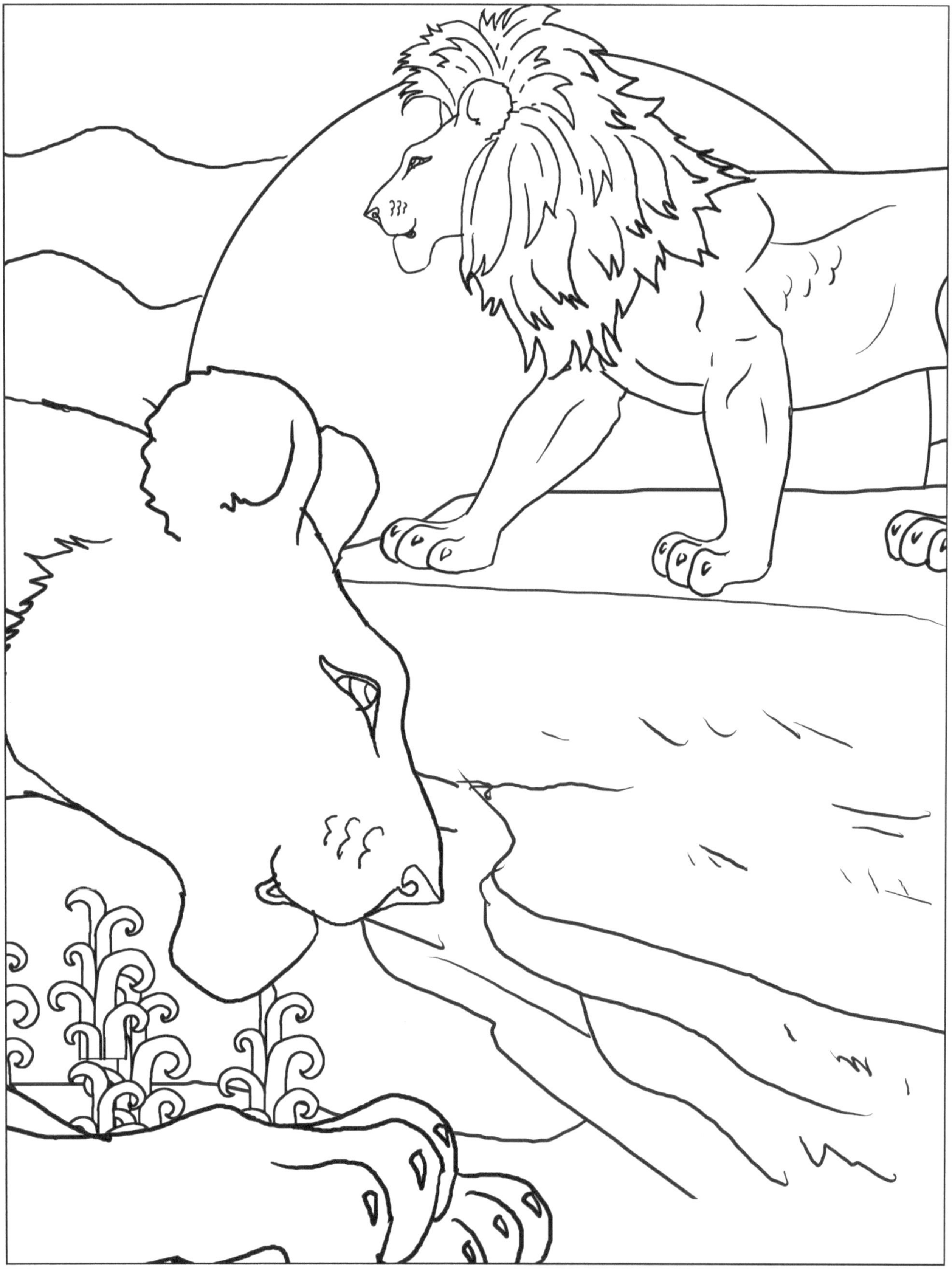

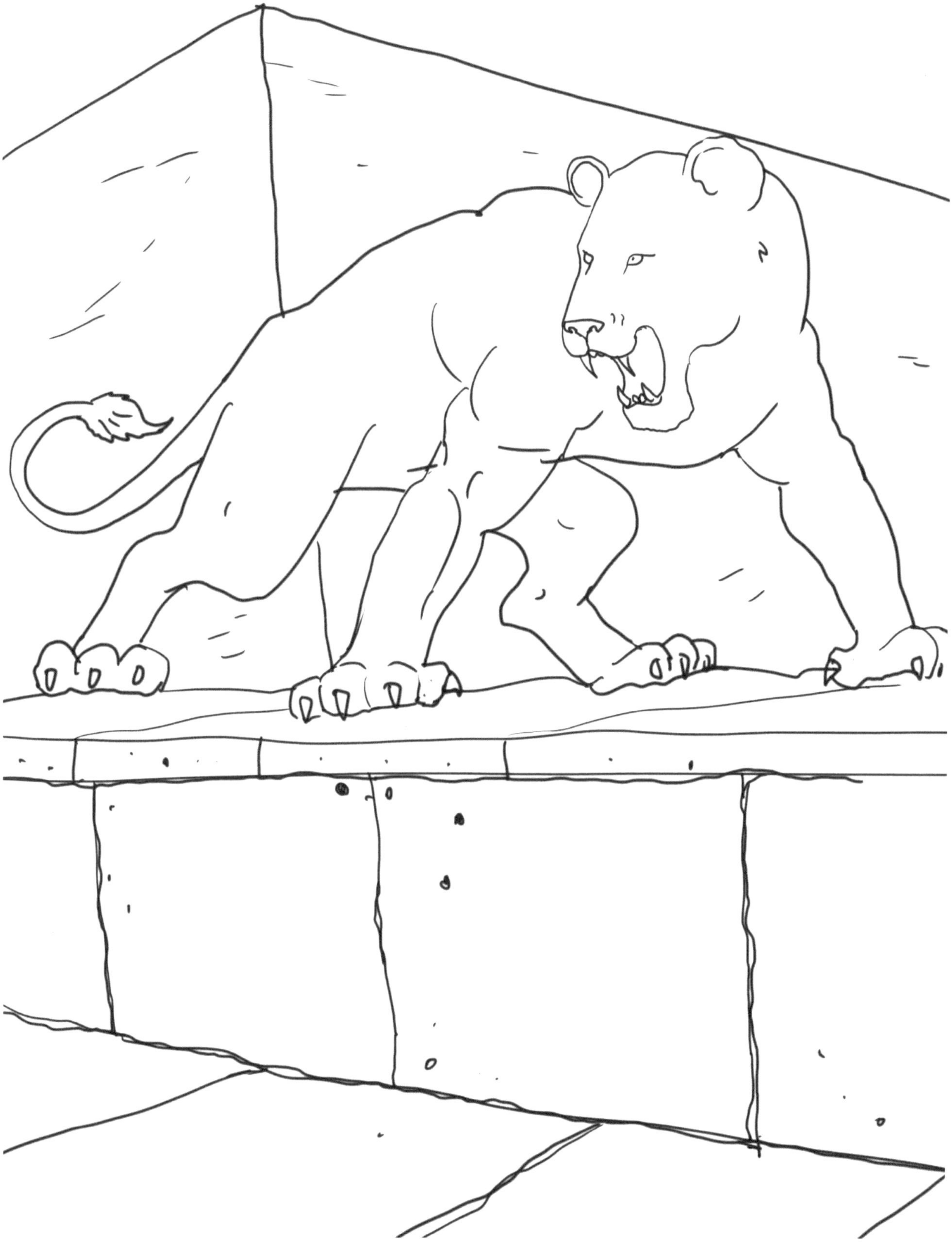

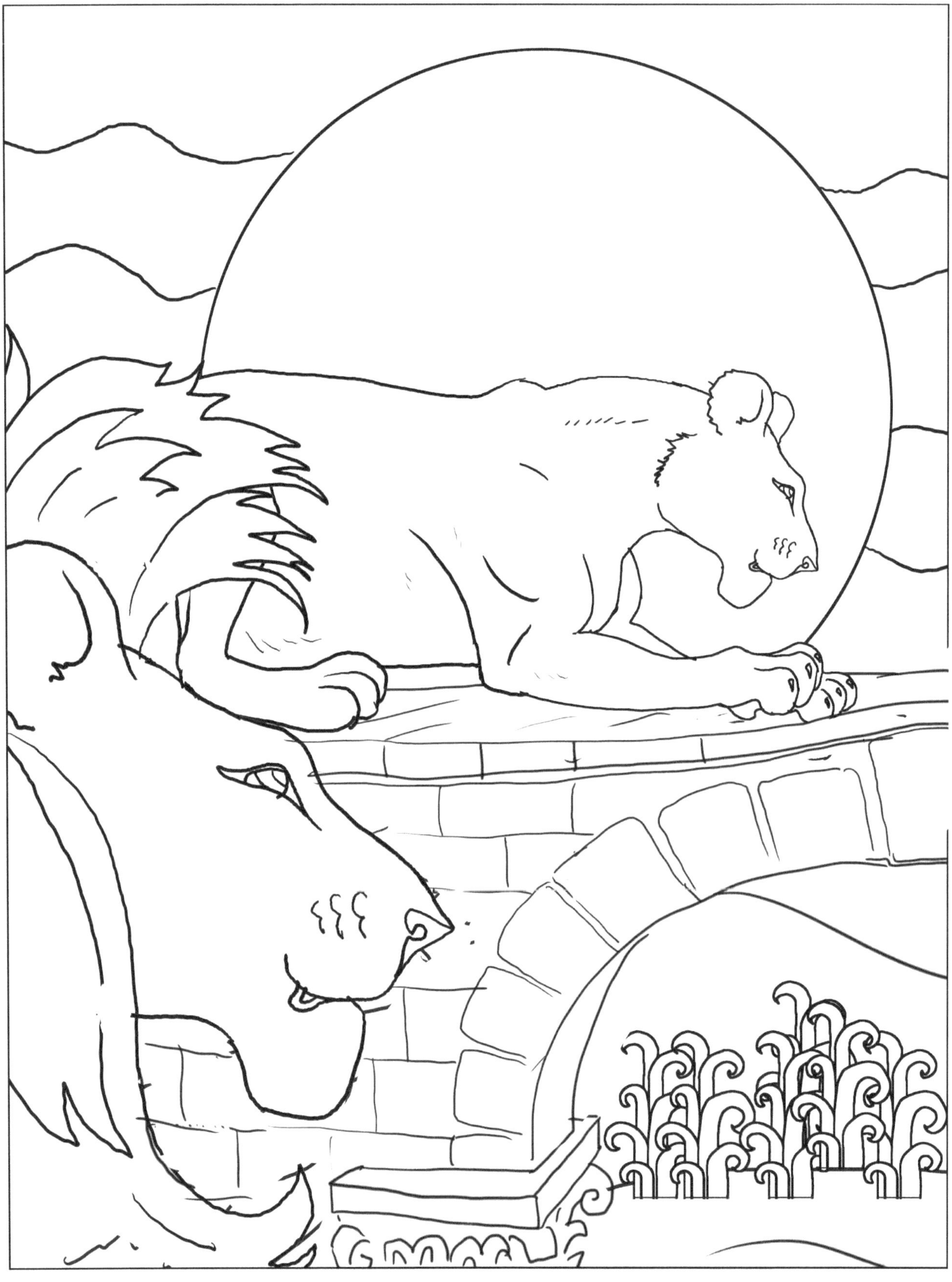

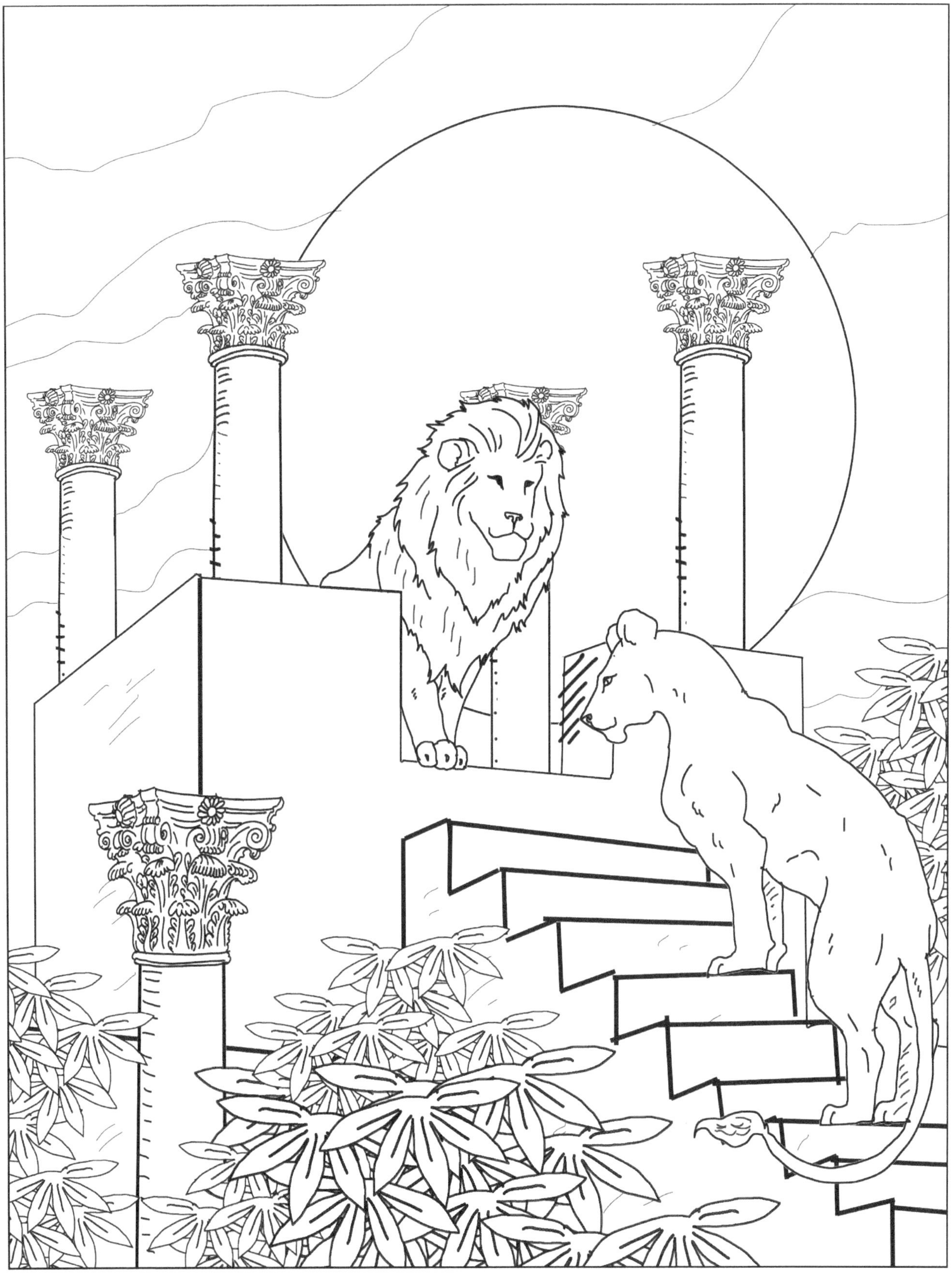

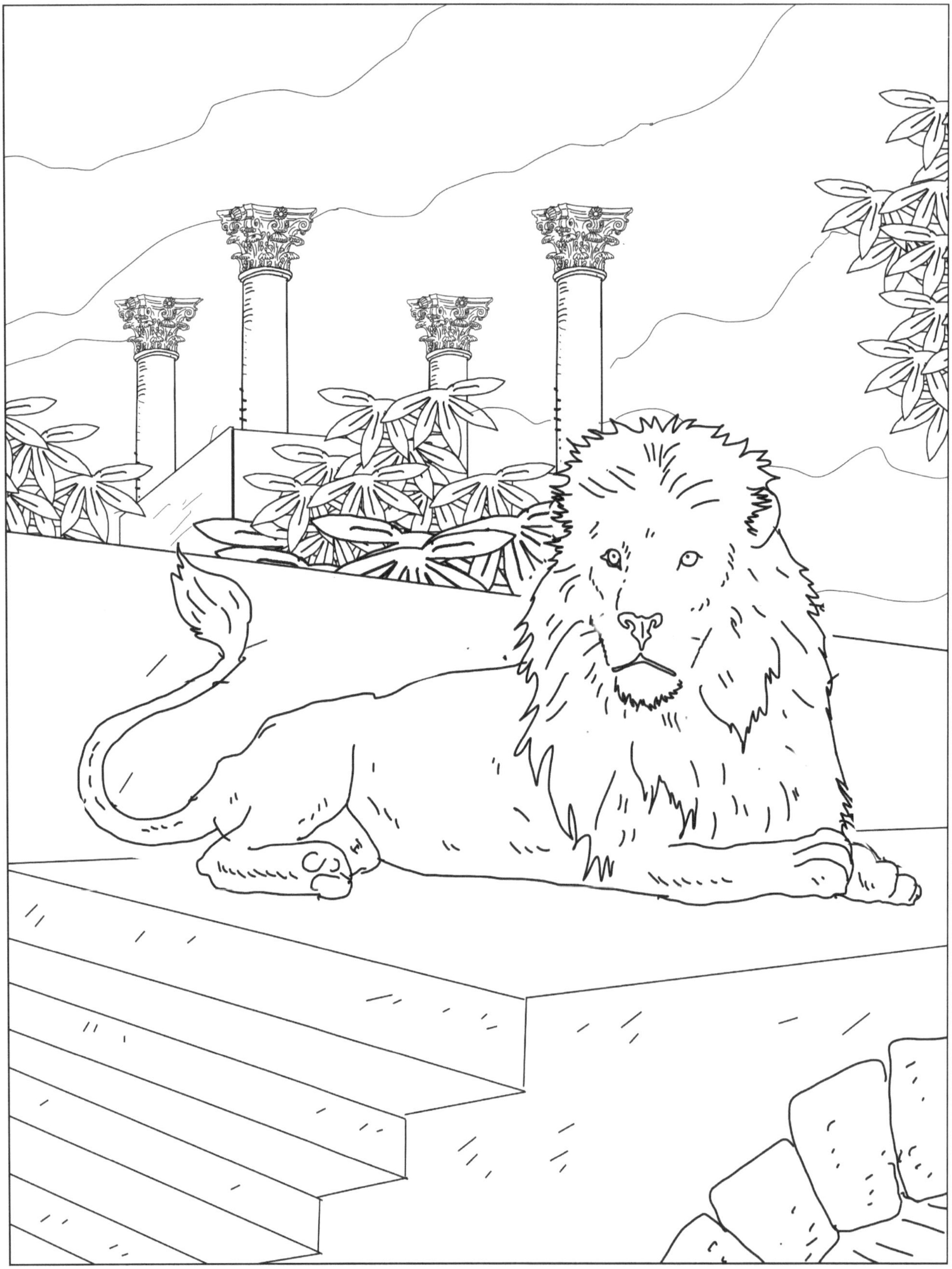

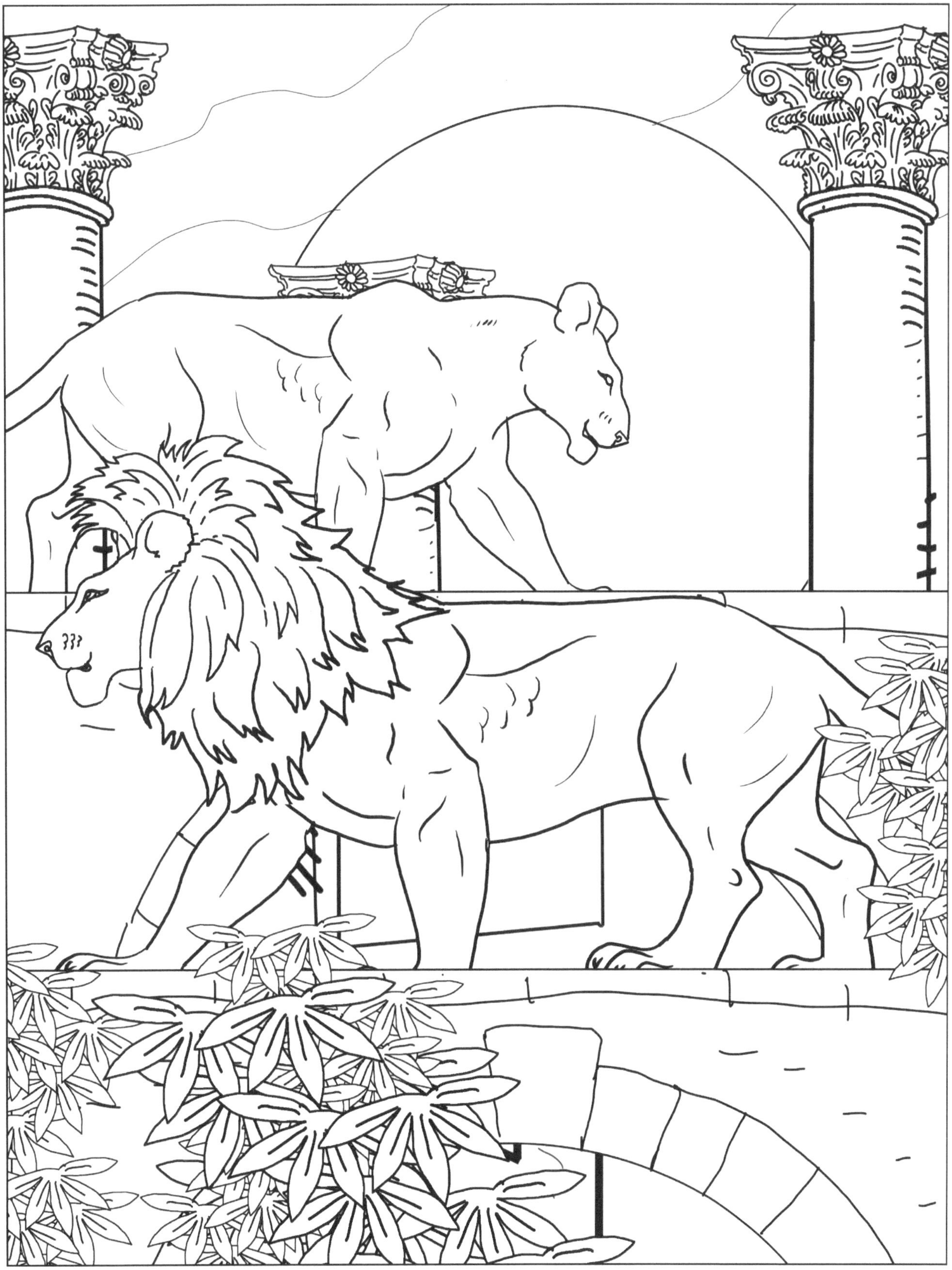

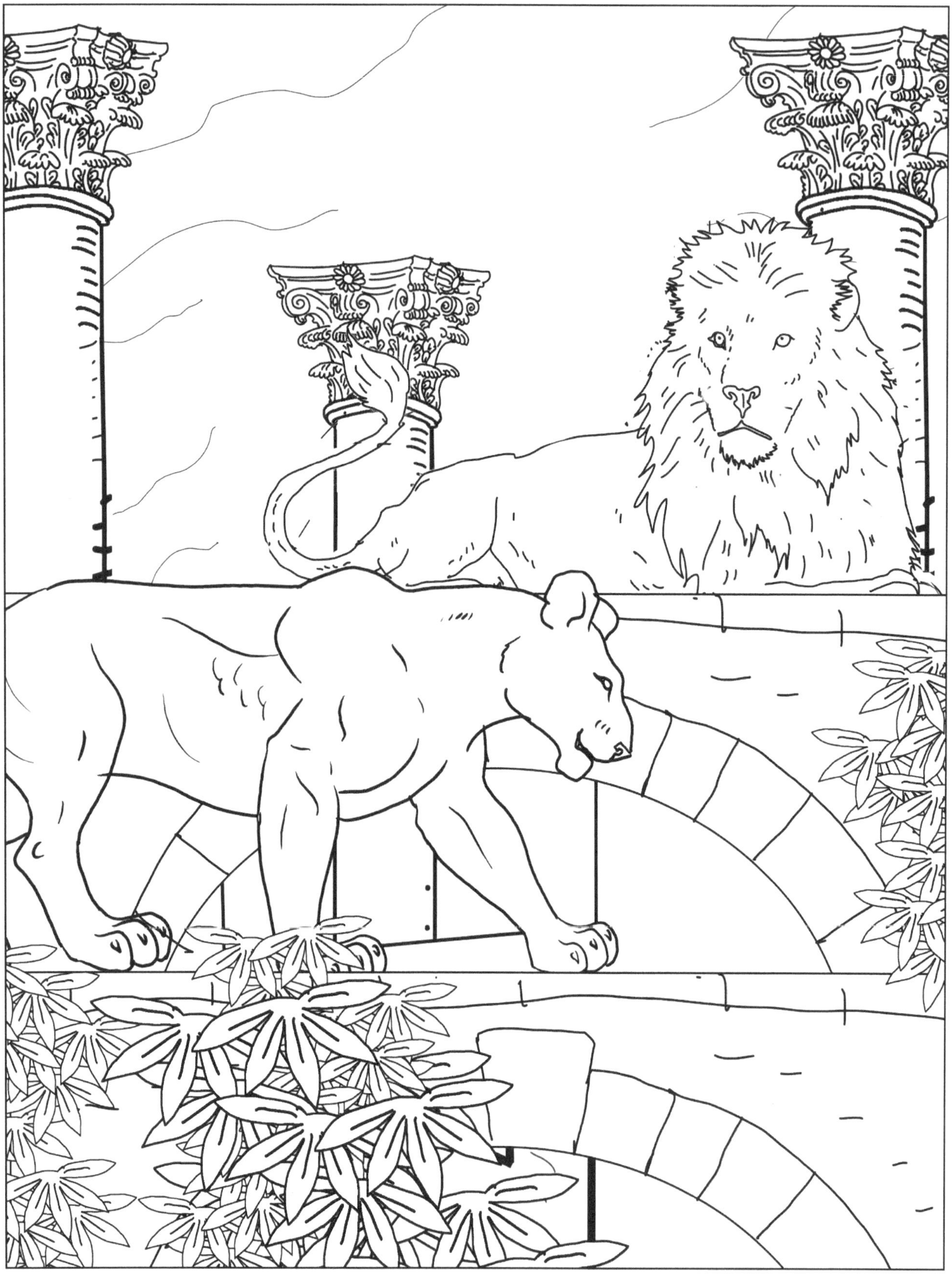

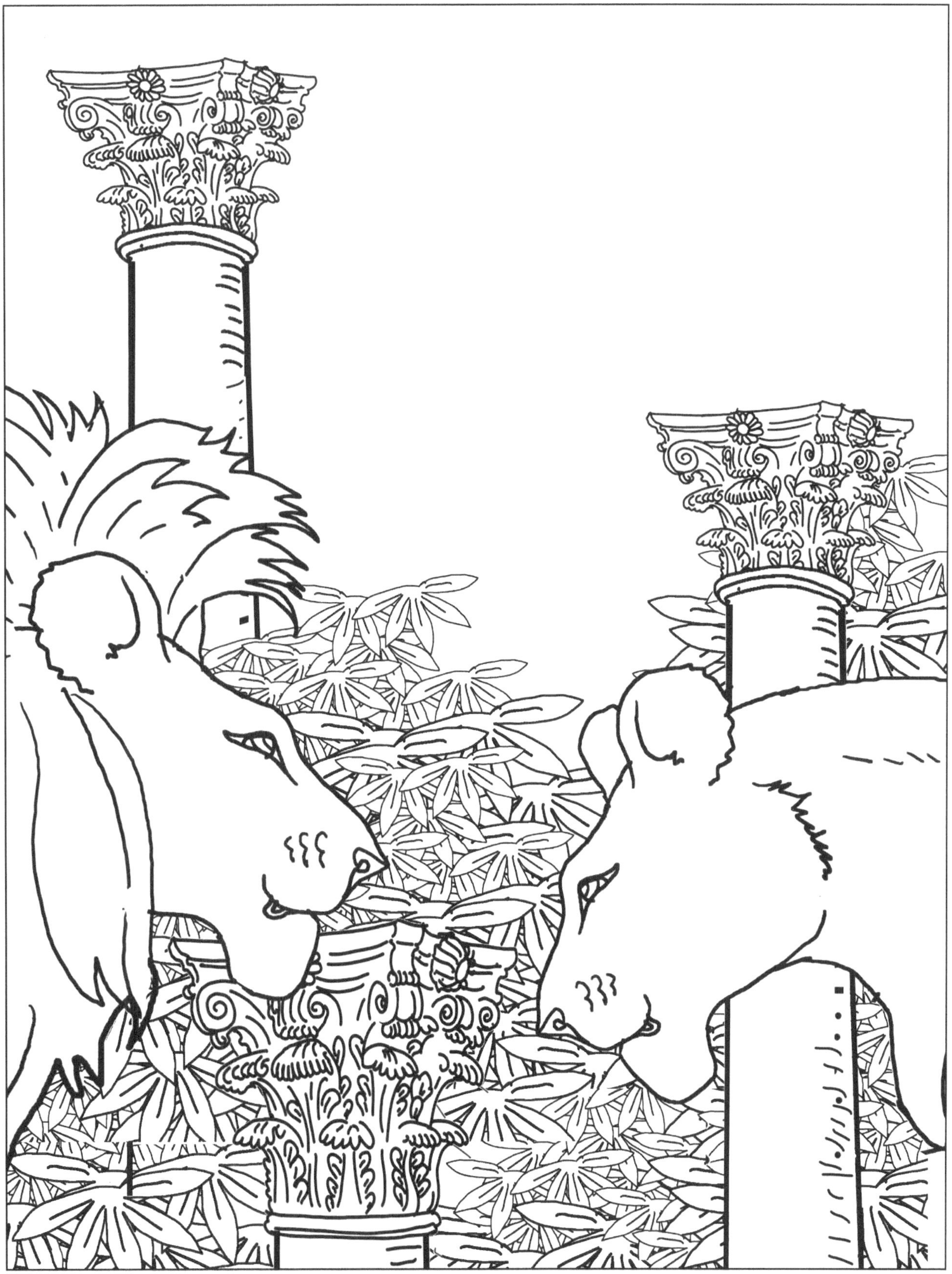

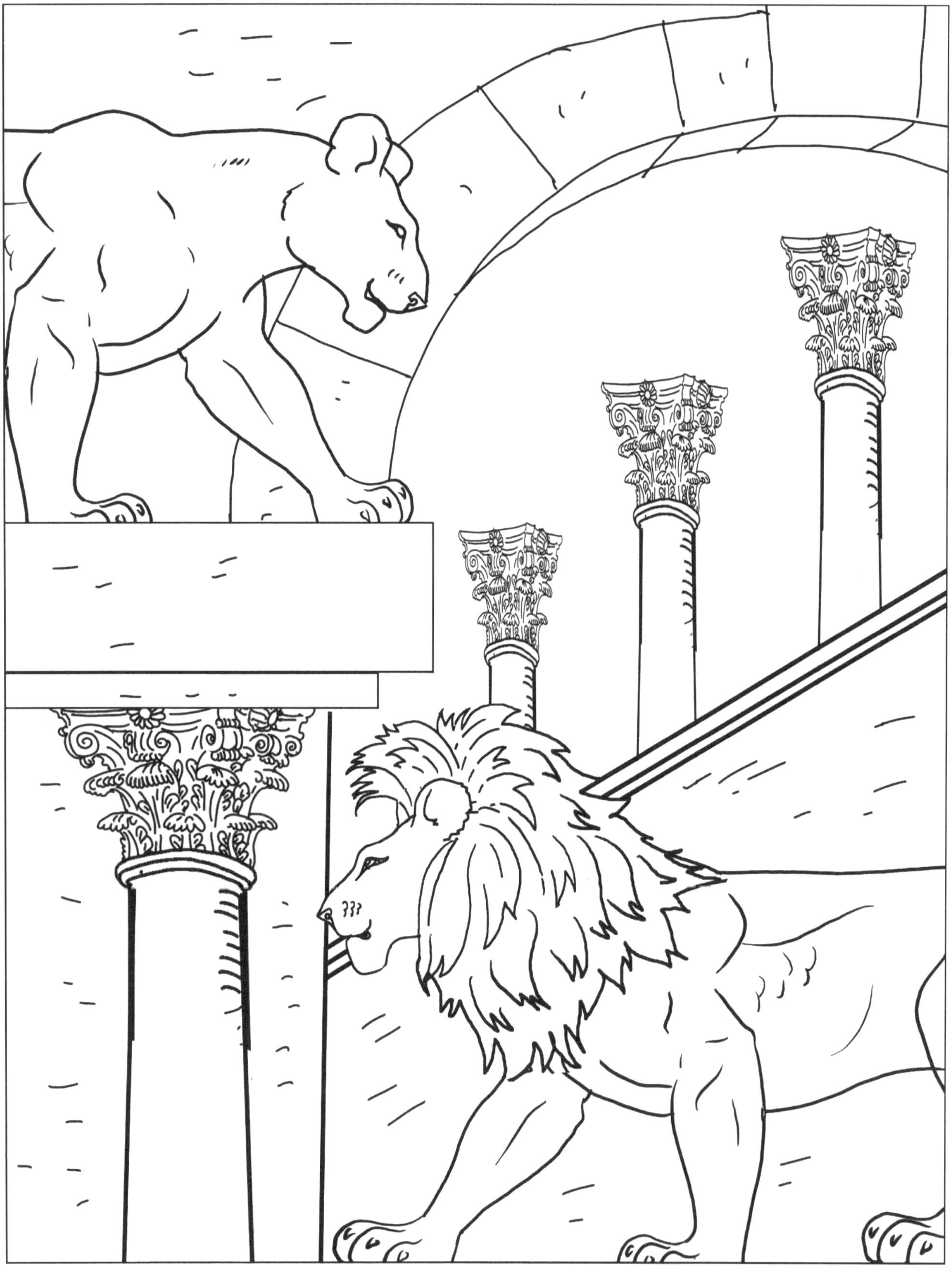

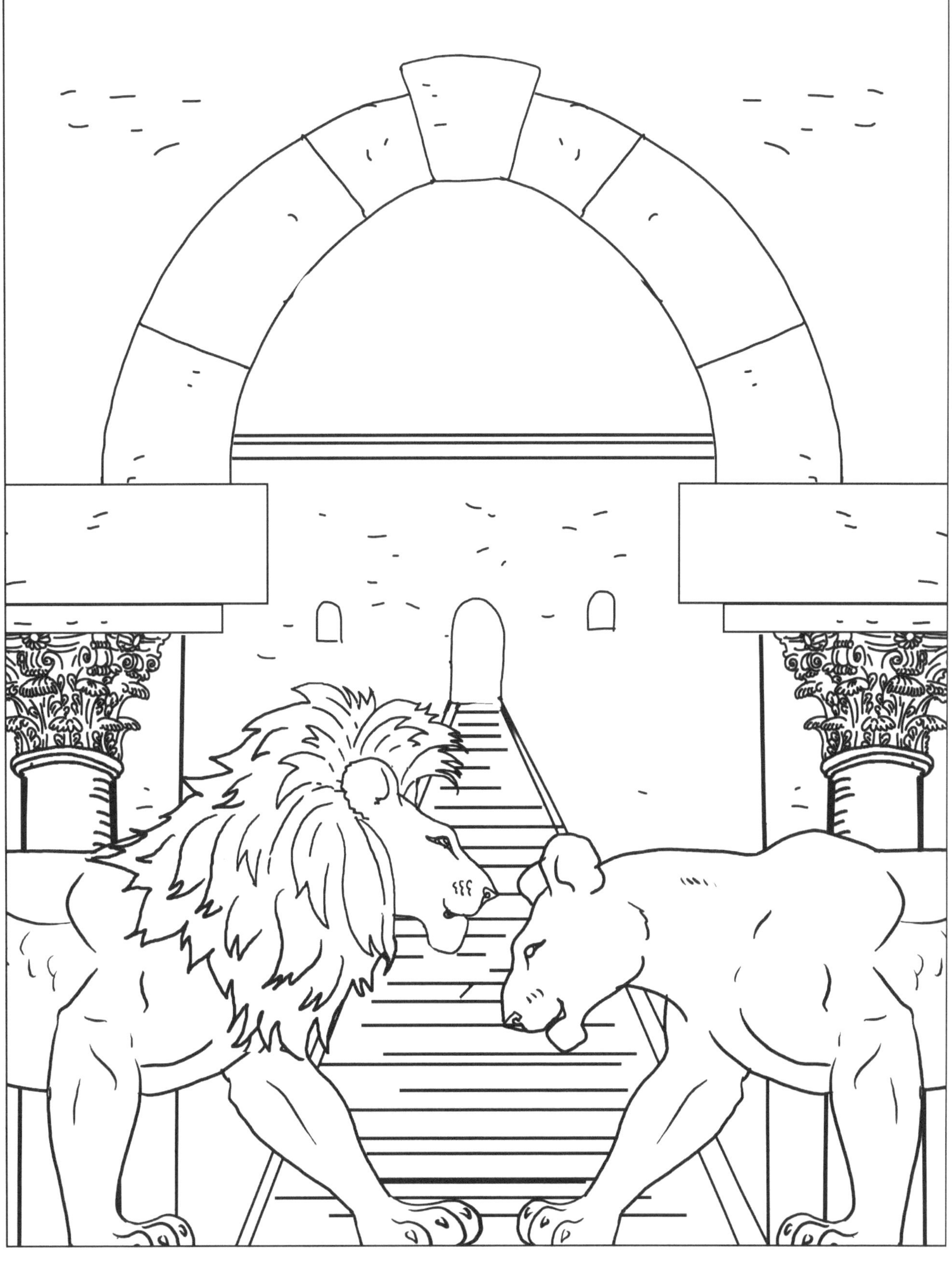

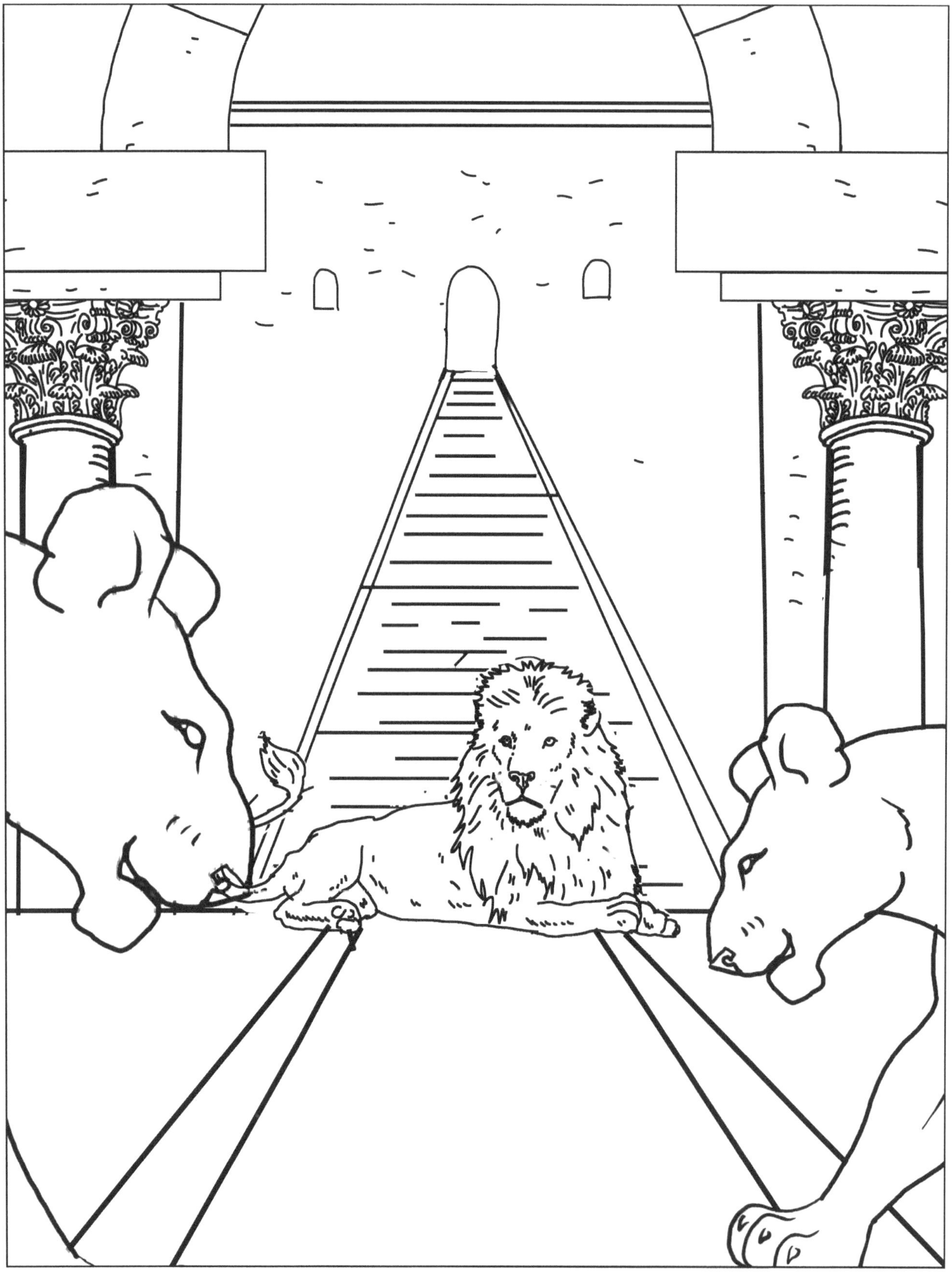

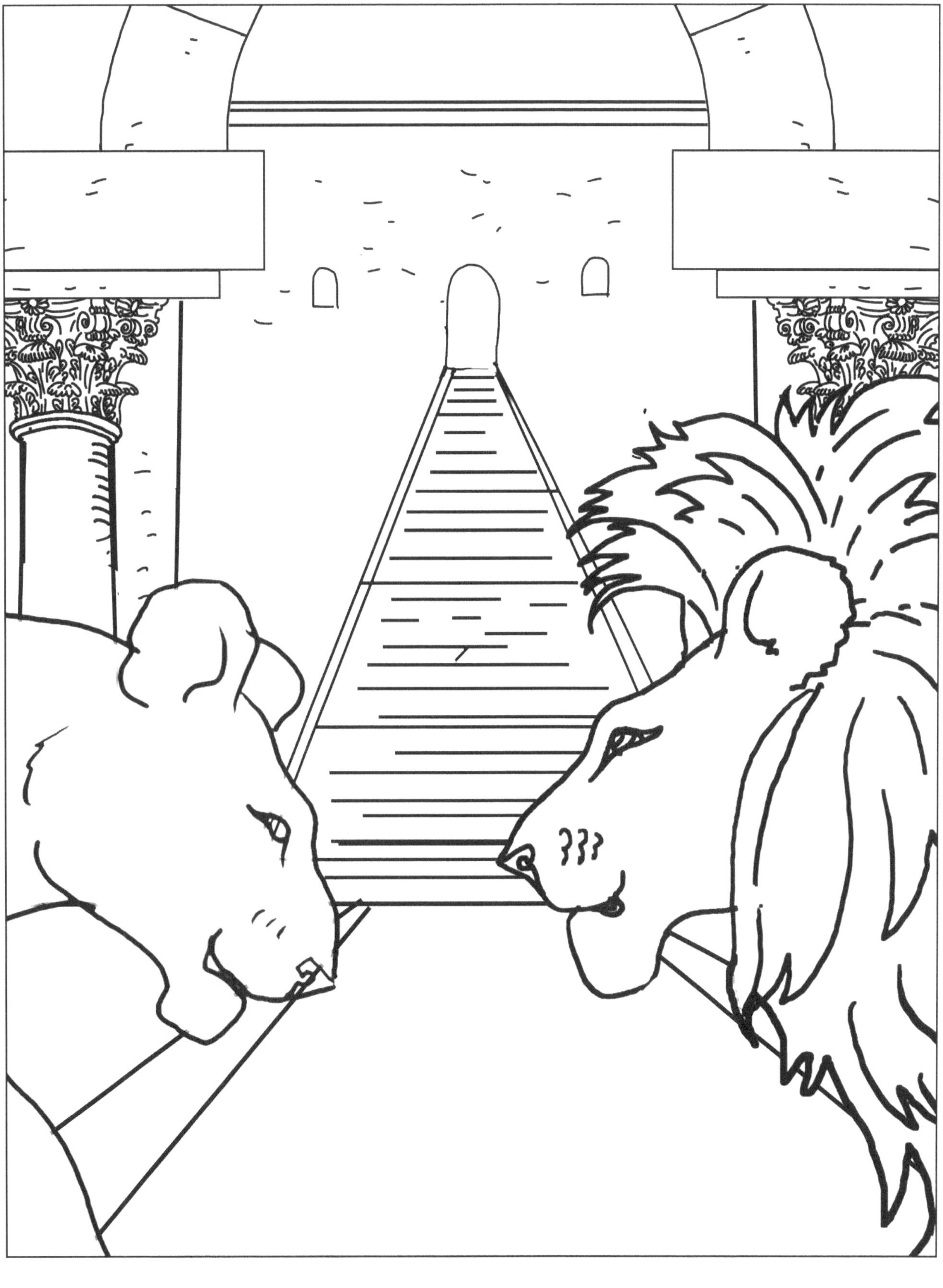

Thank You !

Bambang Wisudyantoro

cannonzhooter@gmail.com

www.ingramcontent.com/pod-product-compliance
Lightning Source LLC
Chambersburg PA
CBHW050425180526
45159CB00005B/2418
* 9 7 8 1 5 3 7 5 0 5 4 7 3 *